A Rainy Day

A Rainy Day

by SANDRA MARKLE

illustrated by CATHY JOHNSON

ORCHARD BOOKS   NEW YORK

Orchard Books, 95 Madison Avenue, New York, NY 10016

Manufactured in the United States of America. Printed by Barton Press, Inc.
Bound by Horowitz/Rae. Book design by Mina Greenstein.
The text of this book is set in 16 point Novarese Medium.
The illustrations are watercolor reproduced in full color.
10 9 8 7 6 5 4 3 2 1

Library of Congress Cataloging-in-Publication Data
Markle, Sandra. A rainy day / by Sandra Markle ; illustrated by Cathy Johnson.   p.   cm.
Summary: Examines simple scientific concepts by observing the effect of raindrops on puddles,
the sky, animals, and the surrounding landscape on a rainy day.
ISBN 0-531-05976-6.   ISBN 0-531-08576-7 (lib. bdg.)
1. Rain and rainfall—Juvenile literature.   [1. Rain and rainfall.]   I. Johnson, Cathy (Cathy A.), ill.
II. Title.   QC924.7.M37 1993   551.57'7—dc20   91-17059

For Jane Anderson, who makes my rainy days sunny.
—S.M.

To Leslie, who made the pictures in my head come alive,
and to Harris, who is always there.
—C.J.

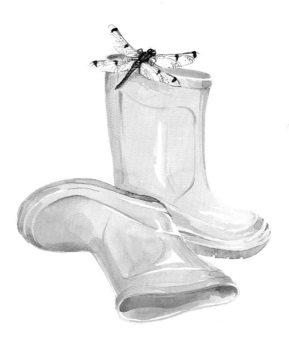

Before it rains, thick gray clouds appear, mounding up or spreading out until they cover the whole sky. The wind may start to blow harder, rattling twigs and rustling leaves. Then the rain begins. Sometimes a few drops turn into a gentle shower. Other times, these first drops warn that a storm with heavy rainfall is on its way.

Few creatures other than ducks and earthworms stay outdoors in the rain. Rain doesn't make ducks wet, because water runs right off their oily feathers. But it soaks through the feathers or fur of many other animals, so they take shelter.

Squirrels and bees, who build homes for themselves, can return to those dry places. Birds may perch under eaves or deep inside bushes. Spiders, crickets, and other bugs hide under bits of bark or leaves.

Earthworms need to be wet to breathe, because air seeps in through their skin only when it's damp. On sunny days, earthworms usually stay underground so their skin will not dry out. Earthworms can't breathe when they are completely underwater, though. On rainy days, when water soaks down into the ground, earthworms come to the surface. Safe from drying out while the rain is falling, they search for food and sometimes seek a mate.

When it rains, some things, such as tree trunks or cement sidewalks, become darker. And some things, such as cars and tree leaves, look shiny. Objects made of cloth, paper, or cardboard change even more when they get wet. A cardboard box left outside during a shower soaks up rainwater like a sponge. As the water dissolves the glue that made the cardboard stiff, the walls of the box sag and wrinkle. Full of water, the cardboard also feels heavier.

Materials such as plastic and rubber don't absorb water this way. Water runs off them the same way it runs off a duck's oily feathers.

People make umbrellas, raincoats, and rain hats out of these materials to protect themselves from the rain. Umbrellas are also made in a dome shape that lets the water run off more easily.

Raindrops that hit the ground bounce. The harder the surface, the higher they rise. When raindrops first strike bare ground, they break loose tiny bits of dirt and rock. More raindrops carry these pieces away, gradually carving holes and grooves in the ground.

When a raindrop strikes the surface of the water in a puddle, pond, lake, or stream, it makes a ringlike wave form. This ring spreads out wider and wider until it finally disappears.

If two raindrops running down a windowpane bump into each other, they join together to make one bigger drop. The same process inside a cloud creates raindrops. Clouds are made up of millions of very tiny water drops. As these drops combine, they get bigger and heavier until they are too heavy to float in the air any longer. Then they fall to the ground as raindrops.

Sometimes, when the sun shines through raindrops, you can see a rainbow. Although sunlight may seem white when it shines through the window and makes a bright patch on the floor, it is really made up of all the colors of light in the rainbow—red, orange, yellow, green, blue, and purple. Like a raindrop, a prism also separates sunlight into these colors.

When sunlight passes through raindrops, the different colors of light slow down—each one to a slightly different speed. This separates the colors, and they become visible as the bands that form the rainbow.

Even after the rain stops, water keeps on falling. It drips off trees and bushes and off the roofs of houses. Some of it soaks into the ground. Just below the surface, a network of shrub and tree roots, grass roots, and flower roots absorbs some of this rainwater. The rest sinks lower, flowing between bits of soil and rock until it reaches bedrock—the hard layer of rock under the soil. There it may collect to form the groundwater tapped by wells, or eventually seep back into streams, ponds, and rivers.

For a while, some water stays on the surface as puddles. But most of the rainwater that does not soak in runs off.

Flowing downhill into ponds and streams
or storm drains, the water ends up in lakes,
reservoirs, or rivers headed for the sea.

Later, the sun's heat will move some of the water that collects in ponds, lakes, and the sea back into the air. There, as millions of tiny droplets, the water forms new clouds.

Eventually, as these tiny drops combine and grow bigger, raindrops will fall once again, and there will be a new rainy day to explore.